Warp and Weft of our lives

H. K. JEJI

Foliohut Press LLC

Copyright by H. K. Jeji
All rights reserved by the author. No part of this work may be reproduced, stored in, or introduced into a retrieval system; or transmitted in any form, or by any means, electronic, recording, photocopying, mechanical, or otherwise, without the prior written permission of the author and the publisher. Translation rights of this work in any language are reserved by the author. The work is subject to a royalty. The work is fully protected under the copyright laws.

Questions can be addressed through the website:
www.foliohutpress.com
Published by Foliohut Press LLC.

This is a work of fiction. Any resemblance to actual persons, living or dead, or actual events is purely coincidental. H. K. Jeji

ISBN 0991396820
ISBN 13 9780991396825
Library of Congress Control Number 2014920412
Foliohut Press LLC
EATON RAPIDS, MI

To my Prajna

ACKNOWLEDGMENTS

Completing this play has been a long journey. I am grateful for my friends whose unwavering support and validation continues to be a constant streak of bright light amid the thick clouds of doubt and stagnation. This journey would not have been possible without Elaine Higden who believed that the story is worth telling and assisted in polishing the manuscript along the way. Rachel Blok provided valuable feedback on the final draft. Sue Perry gave encouragement when it was needed the most and assisted in creating the meaningful cover design.

I would like to give special thanks and gratitude to the great team members at CreateSpace for their patience and support.

CHARACTERS

The following events describe a few days in the lives of three women who are residing in a midsize town in North America. They live in an end unit of a row of town houses.

MRS VIRK. Mother

INDU. Older daughter

SONU. Younger daughter

LAL. Restaurant owner

ANIL. Indu's late husband, never on stage but is spoken of

FATHER. Deceased, never on stage but is spoken of

MRS. SINGH. Ajit's mother, never on stage but is spoken of

AJIT. Mrs. Singh's son, never on stage but is spoken of

SCENE ONE

The sofa set, tables, and table lamps are arranged in center stage so that two sofa armchairs face each other on both ends of the sofa. Along the back side of the sofa, there is a long table with a phone, family pictures, and books.

Along the left center stage wall, there are bookshelves that are filled with books, pictures, and other knick-knacks. A decorative wooden box is tucked away on one of the shelves. Beyond the bookshelves, there is a staircase along the left upstage wall going to the bedrooms. Adjacent to the staircase, there is a hallway leading toward the back of the town house.

Along the right center stage wall, there is a dining table, chairs, and a china cabinet.

There is a kitchen in upstage center. A few feet behind the sofa, there are barstools tucked away underneath the kitchen counter.

There is a TV at an angle so that it can be watched from the sofa and the dining table.

The entire place is tastefully decorated with plants, decorative pieces, and wall hangings.

A basket with yarn and knitting needles is set beside the sofa.

It is Friday evening. There are grocery bags on the kitchen counter. Mrs. Virk is putting away groceries in the kitchen. She is wearing Punjabi clothing. Indu is straightening out things in the living room. She has work clothes on. Sonu is stretched out on the sofa watching television. There are empty pizza boxes and plates on the dining table.

INDU (*taking a deep breath*): I am so full. I should not have eaten so much.

SONU: In my opinion, you should not have eaten the last two servings. You never used to eat this much.

INDU: I still don't. I have a weakness for pizza.

SONU: If you ask me, you have a weakness for chips, doughnuts, and—

MRS. VIRK (*raising her voice*): Sonu, stop it. She works the entire day. She eats only one good meal.

SONU: Mother, it is not good for her.

(*Mrs. Virk brings a tray with cups of tea and places it on the coffee table. She nudges Sonu to fold her legs so that she can sit on the other side of the sofa. Sonu is*

SCENE ONE

changing channels mindlessly. Indu clears the dining table of boxes and dishes.)

MRS. VIRK: Sonu, why don't you leave it on one setting?

(Sonu is drinking tea and still changing channels, but at a slower pace. Indu picks up a cup of tea and sits on the side chair. Silence. All are drinking tea and staring at the television while Sonu keeps changing channels.)

INDU: Mother, try on your clothes we bought today.

SONU *(with excitement)*: Yes, Mother, do try them on.

MRS. VIRK *(hesitantly)*: Oh, all right. But—but I want to wash them first. I never wear new clothes without washing them first. You never know—

INDU: But then we cannot return them.

MRS. VIRK *(surprised)*: Return them! You mean we can take them back and get our money after we brought them home?

SONU: Yes, Mother. Here you can bring clothes home, try them on *(with amusement, circling with her finger)*, and walk around in them. If you do not like them, then you can return them.

INDU: But don't take the price tags off. Just try them on to see if you like them and if you feel comfortable in them.

(*Mrs. Virk takes bags from behind the sofa and exits into the hallway.*)

INDU: Sonu, do you really think I have become a glutton, or were you just joking?

SONU: You never used to eat so much. You are eating too much, as if—as if someone is after you.

INDU: No wonder all of my pants are so tight. I thought Mother had been putting them in the dryer even after I told her not to do so.

SONU (*disinterested*): There is nothing interesting coming on the television.

INDU: Why don't you read a book?

SONU: Let us see the late movie in the theater.

INDU: I have to go to work tomorrow.

SONU: On Saturday?

INDU: I am filling in for somebody else.

SONU: Oh!

(*Mrs. Virk enters. She has pants and a shirt on. She looks a bit uncomfortable. Sonu jumps up from the sofa. She puts her arm under Mrs. Virk's arm and steps forward along with her as if showing her off.*)

MRS. VIRK (*gently warding her off*): Oh, silly girl, stop.

INDU: Mother, you look beautiful.

SONU: I must say that I selected the right style and color. Just perfect! (*She steps back and watches her.*)

INDU: Mother, from now on, you must wear these when you go out.

MRS. VIRK: Not all the time?

INDU: At least in the stores. Next, you must learn to drive. You must take a written test. Then, I will teach you how to drive.

SONU: What about me?

INDU: What about you?

(*Indu collects the cups from the table and takes them into the kitchen. The clatter of the dishes being washed is heard in the background. Mrs. Virk exits toward the hallway.*)

SONU (*raising her voice*): If you do not teach me, I will find a way.

(*Indu returns and is standing near Sonu.*)

INDU: I am sure you will. I will teach you in due time. Don't worry. But first, you must pass the written test.

SONU: Why does there have to be a time line for everything?

(*There is silence. Mrs. Virk returns. She has changed her clothes. She picks up her knitting and settles down in the chair.*)

MRS. VIRK (*knitting*): God willing, this summer, I will start teaching, teaching or tutoring—

INDU: Teaching?

MRS. VIRK: Yes, teaching! (*She is knitting.*)

SONU: Mom, what do you know about teaching?

MRS. VIRK: I used to teach before I got married.

INDU: I did not know that.

SONU: Where? In a small room, in a remote village?

MRS. VIRK: In a private school, in my town. (*Addressing Sonu*) And it is not a small town. (*Pause.*) I will

SCENE ONE

start in the basement of the temple. In the beginning, maybe tutoring. Later on, I may add dancing classes.

SONU: Now, that I can see! Mother teaching dance classes.

INDU: This is good news, Mother. I am so happy for you. Father would have been so proud of you. He would have liked this rather than your... (*Sonu is giving Indu a stern look for bringing up their father. The moment Indu realizes it, she stops.*)

MRS. VIRK: Yes, I guess he would have. He used to say if I wanted to, I could go back to teaching, but I never did. I never did.

SONU: How did this come about, Mother, all of a sudden, you want to be a teacher?

MRS. VIRK: It didn't happen all of a sudden. Mrs. Singh suggested it a few months ago. Since then, I have been thinking about it.

INDU: Mother, I am so happy for you.

MRS. VIRK: But all that is a few months away. Remember, a few days ago, I mentioned working at the Tikki restaurant.

INDU (*unnerved*): Yes, Mother, you did. And I told you there is no need for you to work there.

(*Indu looks disturbed and distant. She goes upstairs.*)

Sonu (*irritated*): Work! Work! All discussions center around work. Either they begin with work or they end with work. Both of you have nothing else to say. All the time…work…work, as if there is nothing more to life than work.

Mrs. Virk: We would be on the streets without her work!

Sonu: What does she do beside work?

Mrs. Virk (*dismayed*): What else can she do? By the time she comes home, she is tired. Without her work, where would you be?

Sonu (*annoyed*): All right, Mother! Why don't you join her; find work for yourself. All she does is stand at the cashier's desk and scan the bar codes. You seem to make a big deal out of it, as if — as if she was lifting bricks all day. You don't hear her complaining.

Mrs. Virk: If it is so easy, why don't you try it for one day?

Sonu (*incensed*): Didn't I say I will?

Mrs. Virk: When?

SCENE ONE

Sonu: This Monday!

Mrs. Virk: Why not tomorrow? She is going to work tomorrow. Go with her. She has mentioned that she can ask for a few hours of work at her store.

Sonu (*raising her voice with irritation*): I will, Mother. I will! If I work, I want to work in the mall and not in that store where I have to wear that funny uniform all day.

Mrs. Virk (*with surprise and enthusiasm*): So you have been asking around for a job already. How silly of me! You go to the mall all the time. Why didn't you tell me? You silly girl!

Sonu: Oh, Mother, I have not found any job yet. It is just an idea. If I have to work, I might as well work at a decent place.

Mrs. Virk (*with frustration*): And who is offering you a job there?

Sonu: Ajit's cousin works in the mall! She can find a job for me.

Mrs. Virk: That little girl? Mrs. Singh said she works there through some school program. And it is only a summer job.

Sonu: Mother, you—sometimes you talk as if you know everything.

Mrs. Virk (*exasperated*): I know more than you do, and I am sensing that you have no intention of working.

Sonu (*offended*): I said I will, didn't I? So I will. If you want me to go with her tomorrow, then I will go with her.

Mrs. Virk (*getting up and collecting the tray*): You are a stubborn girl. It will be a year soon…sitting around—

Sonu (*raising her voice*): What, Mother? You do not trust me? Do you want me to get ready and sit in the car now? I said I will go with her in the morning, and I will.

Mrs. Virk (*in a low and withdrawn voice*): Oh, hush, girl! I have heard all this before. (*She leaves and returns after putting the tray on the kitchen counter.*)

(*Indu enters. She has changed from her work clothes.*)

Mrs. Virk: Indu, I forgot to tell you that Lal is coming to pick me up.

Sonu: Who?

Mrs. Virk: The owner of Tikki restaurant.

Sonu (*disinterested*): Oh!

SCENE ONE

INDU (*gives Mrs. Virk a frightened look*): Here? Now?

MRS. VIRK: It is not what you think.

INDU: Then, what?

MRS. VIRK: His mother is here for a visit. She wants to see me. Just for an hour or so. (*Pause*.) They wanted to invite us for dinner. I said no. I said you are busy. I know how you feel.

INDU (*angrily*): Do you, Mother?

(*The phone rings. Sonu picks up the phone. After listening, she puts the receiver aside.*)

SONU (*rushing upstairs*): I will take it upstairs.

(*Indu listens for a moment, then hangs up the phone.*)

MRS. VIRK (*hastily*): I better get ready. (*She goes upstairs.*)

(*A knock on the door is heard. Indu steps toward the hallway to see who is at the door. Lal enters, rushing in.*)

LAL (*looks around, uneasily*): The door is unlocked.

INDU (*surprised*): You!

LAL (*moving toward her*): I see you are still angry with me. You have not forgiven me.

INDU (*stepping away*): There is nothing to forgive. I want you to stay away from my family and my house.

LAL: I want to help.

INDU: You have done enough. Stay away from my sister.

LAL: I am not that kind of person.

INDU: What kind are you? You must stay away from my family.

LAL: Our families have known each other for a long time; my one mistake. (*He moves toward her. Indu moves away from him. Once again, he steps toward Indu and has a faint smile on his face.*) My one mistake! You have a big heart. Forgive me. Besides, you are in this country now. You don't have to be living like a nun. People won't believe it anyway. Who cares about this sort of thing here?

INDU: I care. You have a daughter. Ask her if she would care in the same situation. She is old enough, as you say in this country. (*Pause.*) In this country, children grow up very fast.

SCENE ONE

LAL (*steps toward Indu*): Here, here—

INDU (*retreating*): Evil is evil and wrong is wrong... in all corners of the world. (*Agitated*) I am telling you once and for all, stay away, especially from my sister.

LAL (*moving toward Indu*): It was just that you...

INDU (*stepping away*): I won't hesitate to tell your wife.

LAL (*laughing*): Do you think she will believe you?

INDU: I will tell my mother.

LAL: Listen, what good would it do? This can remain our little secret.

INDU: You don't know me.

LAL: This country...

INDU: You think morality gets washed away when you cross the oceans or when you step outside your house?

LAL (*moving toward her*): It was not that bad. I am not a monster. (*Chuckling*) I am an honorable family man, an honorable, hardworking family man.

INDU: As I said, I won't hesitate to tell your wife.

(*Lal rushes toward her and tries to hold Indu's arm. She manages to escape his grasp.*)

LAL (*amused*): There is no need to be that way. I was merely suggesting to your mother that both of them can work in the restaurant until things get better. They have been in this country for almost a year now. (*With concern*) Things must be difficult for you. I mean, you have to support the entire household by yourself. I just want to help.

(*Indu walks away and stops at the foot of the stairs as Mrs. Virk comes downstairs all dressed up. Lal presses his palms and tries to touch her feet. However, she stops him midway and touches his shoulder. He shows her respect. She returns that with her blessings in the traditional way.*)

MRS. VIRK (*charmed by him*): May God give you a long life, Son. (*Turning toward Indu*) Indu, come with us.

LAL: Yes, Indu, why don't you?

INDU: Sonu and I have other plans, Mother.

MRS. VIRK (*surprised*): I did not know.

LAL: Then, shall we go, Auntie?

MRS. VIRK: Sit down, Son. I will bring tea.

LAL: No, no, Auntie. It is all right. No need for formality. They are waiting for us.

MRS. VIRK: Now, it is no bother. (*She exits to the kitchen.*)

LAL: My mother remembers you very fondly.

INDU (*without looking at him*): Does she?

(*Mrs. Virk is standing in the kitchen and leaning over the counter.*)

MRS. VIRK (*raising her voice*): Son, I have told Indu many times...how far back our families go. I remember your grandfather coming to our house...what a gracious man. And your father, may God rest his soul, what an untimely parting...very honorable man.

(*There is silence. Mrs. Virk brings a tray with tea and cookies. While she is pouring tea, she continues.*) Yes, as I was saying. I have explained to Indu that our family ties go far back, many generations.

LAL: Yes, Auntie, Mother often talks about the generosity of your late husband. What an untimely loss!

MRS. VIRK: Whatever is God's will. (*Looking at Indu*) It is Indu's situation—losing a husband at such a young age. Fate has played its ugly hand. It is unbearable for a mother to see her daughter struggling by herself. (*Sniffles.*)

LAL: Auntie, I will—

INDU: Mother, don't keep them waiting.

MRS. VIRK (*ignoring Indu*): Yes, Son, that was noble of you, assisting in the time of need. She was so far away from family, in a foreign country…very noble of you.

LAL (*getting up*): Auntie Ji, Mother is waiting for us, we must—

MRS. VIRK: Yes, Son, yes. (*She hurriedly collects empty dishes and exits to kitchen.*)

(*Lal is looking at Indu. Indu is staring at the muted television. Mrs. Virk returns, for a second. She watches and weighs the situation.*)

MRS. VIRK: Indu, why don't you come with us?

(*Indu looks at Mrs. Virk in silence.*)

MRS. VIRK (*promptly*): I forgot, you and Sonu have plans.

(*Mrs. Virk nods her head with awkwardness. Lal holds his palms together toward Indu, but she does not respond. Mrs. Virk and Lal exit. Indu, shaking, takes her father's picture and holds it in front of her.*)

INDU: Plans! Plans! What plans? What have I done?

Oh, Father! What have I done, what have I done to myself? Whatever you tried to do for me, I have undone it with the stroke of a pen. Give me strength, God, let me step out of this circle…and I promise I will never look back again. (*She folds her arms around the picture and curls up on the sofa.*)

Curtain.

SCENE TWO

It is Saturday late afternoon. Mrs. Virk is seen in the kitchen washing dishes. Indu is straightening out things on the dining table. Mrs. Virk returns to the living room. She sits on the sofa chair and starts knitting. Indu returns to the sofa with a book and begins to read.

MRS. VIRK: For all the newspapers and books he read, he didn't have much to say, did he? If I write down what he said throughout his life, it wouldn't even fill one sheet of paper.

INDU: But, Mother, he loved you.

MRS. VIRK: Maybe.

INDU: He took care of you.

MRS. VIRK: So he did.

INDU: You knew when he was happy.

MRS. VIRK: Oh, yes, his face would light up, his eyes would sparkle, and his cheeks would swell up. You could see it through his beard. Oh, yes, you could see he was happy.

INDU: You could see when he was annoyed or when he didn't like something.

SCENE TWO

MRS. VIRK: Oh, yes! You would know from the length of his walk. He would pace on that veranda or walk along those railway tracks for hours. Yes, you knew.

INDU: Mother, you could feel his anger, his frustration, and his joy, but not his love...not his love!

MRS. VIRK (*annoyed*): I guess he did love me in his own way.

INDU: Yes, he did, in his own way! And what is your way, Mother?

MRS. VIRK: What do you mean? Didn't I take care of you...clothes, meals, appearance?

INDU: The servants did all that, Mother.

MRS. VIRK: Well, they couldn't have done it without me. The servants do not lift a finger without someone instructing them all the time.

INDU: You think so! Father would have done so.

MRS. VIRK: Done what?

INDU: Instructed the servants. We were not dolls to be decorated and let go. I was your daughter. I needed attention, your affection.

MRS. VIRK: Oh, you had attention, the love.

INDU: What are you talking about, Mother?

MRS. VIRK: You had plenty of love from the day you were born.

INDU: Not from you!

MRS. VIRK: From the day you were born, I ceased to exist for him. (*Sniffles*) He never looked at me the same way ever again. You had him from the day you were born. You had him for the rest of the years.

INDU: What a cruel thing to say to your own daughter!

MRS. VIRK: I dressed up for him. I arranged parties for him. I invited all his friends. I managed the household for him. It seemed the more I tried, the more he withdrew, the more distant he became. You had him all these years. And I watched and I cringed. You had him all these years.

INDU: Stop it, Mother. Do not be so cruel.

MRS. VIRK: I did love him. But he—

INDU: He was a human being, Mother. We all have our shortcomings, but we tend to justify or ignore them if we love the person. We tend to dwell on them and magnify them if we do not like the person.

MRS. VIRK: I did love him, but—

SCENE TWO

INDU: He loved you the way you are; he ignored your frivolities. He never sanctioned you with words, actions, or expressions.

MRS. VIRK: I took care of the household.

INDU: The servants did that.

(*Silence.*)

INDU: You with your words, actions, and expressions would let the person know of your disdain. In fact, Mother, you will not stop until you hammer the nails through the person's psyche. Mother, you and your games, you think he did not see through them? You talk about love. What is love to you—a mere fleeting fancy?

MRS. VIRK (*sniffles*): It is not true. It is not true at all!

INDU: He could hear your whispers and see your gestures. Mother, let it go. He is dead. For God's sake, let him rest in peace. And I am sorry for whatever you think I did to you.

MRS. VIRK: It was you—

INDU: Mother, stop it. I am your daughter…his daughter. For God's sake, stop it. Let him rest in peace. Don't be heartless.

MRS. VIRK: When you came here, I thought, now, he will be all mine. Not even two years passed...he was dead. What luck!

INDU: All he talked about was you. "How is your mother? Is she all right?" You shut him out of your life. What was he supposed to do? You were busy with your parties, your trips to the market, and your friends. There was no place for him.

MRS. VIRK (*softening up*): Did he talk about me? He inquired about me!

INDU: All the time.

MRS. VIRK: Oh! (*Crying, wiping her eyes*) Oh, he did love me. He did, didn't he?

INDU: Yes, Mother, he did (*comforting her*). Here, here, now stop this.

(*Sonu comes downstairs in a hurry. She is casually dressed to go out.*)

SONU: Stop bickering, you two. Stop it! He is dead. He has been dead for years. Stop it.

MRS. VIRK: All right! All right! All I wanted to say is that I did my best by him, by both of you. Here, I have said my peace once and for all. I did my best. (*Sniffles.*)

SCENE TWO

Sonu: Mother, I am going to the mall.

Mrs. Virk: I thought you had headache.

Sonu (*annoyed*): I had headache this morning. That's why I could not get up, Mother!

Mrs. Virk: When will you return?

Sonu: Do you know how many stores there are in the mall?

Mrs. Virk: You don't have to go to each one of them. Nothing has changed since yesterday.

Sonu: Now, what did you use to say? "Let us go and look at the new designs, new colors." Everything is inside, under one roof. It is not that I have to walk outside in the heat or cold. Remember how we used to wander from store to store in that scorching sun, dragging our umbrellas from store to store? Remember, Mother—you and I?

Mrs. Virk: Oh, be quiet. Those were different times. When will you return?

Sonu: I do not know.

Mrs. Virk: What do you mean?

(*In the background, a car stops with a screech of tires. The horn is heard.*)

Sonu: I don't know. Later on, we may go to the movies. Bye.

(*Mrs. Virk was about to say something, but Sonu rushes out the door. Mrs. Virk goes after her in haste. Indu looks up and then turns to the book. Mrs. Virk returns to her seat and resumes her knitting.*)

Mrs. Virk (*irritated*): That girl does not know about the world. She gives me many sleepless nights. In this foreign land—

Indu: She knows plenty. She is not a child.

Mrs. Virk: Oh, she is, she certainly is, growing up without a father when she really needed him. (*She settles down in her seat and untangles the knitting yarn.*)

Indu: You did very well. As far as Father is concerned, when did you ever listen to his advice? He was there for the world to see. You never listened to him.

Mrs. Virk: I did listen to him. I did. I listened to him as much as a wife should listen to a husband. I was a devoted wife. The only thing I did not do was hide my face in books.

Indu: You were always too busy with your parties and clubs.

MRS. VIRK: Why are you bringing all that up now?

INDU: You did. You are always talking about him as if you loved him or cared for him.

MRS. VIRK: I was a good wife and a good mother. I was—

INDU (*interrupting*): Mother, please, leave these stories alone.

MRS. VIRK: I see you are hurting. I wish I could do something for you. As I mentioned the other day, I am ready to work. I do not want to be a burden on you. I never wanted… (*sniffles*).

INDU: Mother, you are not a burden on me.

MRS. VIRK: I can see sorrow in your eyes. After your marriage, I thought one responsibility is over and one is left. Somehow, God will take care of everything. Your father was alive. I do not know what bad deeds I have done. In my old age, I have two daughters to worry about.

INDU: You do not have to worry about me, Mother.

MRS. VIRK: You do not know how I cry for you. So talented, so beautiful, and what luck! God is punishing me. When your father heard about Anil's heart attack, he did not get out of bed for two days. After that—after that, he lost the will to live. For the last two years of his life, he was an empty vessel...just a shell of a man. I wish he had taken me with him. I do not know why God is punishing me.

INDU: This is my life! How is God punishing you?

MRS. VIRK: God punishes parents through the lives of their children. In a way, he was the lucky one; he didn't have to witness this. (*Sniffling*.)

INDU: You think it is good that he is dead?

MRS. VIRK (*horrified*): Oh, I am not saying that at all. How can you say such a thing?

INDU: Then what are you saying, Mother?

MRS. VIRK: What I mean to say is that he doesn't have to see this—

INDU: What is *this*, Mother? What is *this*?

MRS. VIRK: Oh, why do you have to be so—

INDU: What? What am I?

MRS. VIRK: Why are you so bitter? So young and so bitter, but then you have always been like that.

INDU: Like what? What have I been like?

MRS. VIRK: You never cared for me, not the way a daughter should.

INDU: And what way is that, Mother?

MRS. VIRK: Oh, I do not mean, "care for" in the sense of "taking care of." There was no need for that. There were servants around all the time, and your father provided for everything. I mean you never asked me for advice — what to wear, how to dress up. You never went to the movies with me or visited family and friends. You never did. You were never interested in any of those things.

INDU: You never asked me, Mother. You never asked me to go along with you. You were too busy with your parties and clubs.

MRS. VIRK: You always stayed behind, on the sides, watching...always watching.

INDU: You were too busy for me, Mother. Always busy.

MRS. VIRK: You were always watching. I can still picture you in your frock, your braids hanging on the shoulders with silk ribbons, always watching —

INDU: You are talking about me as if I were a ghost watching you.

MRS. VIRK (*to herself*): Always watching.

INDU: You never asked me to come with you.

MRS. VIRK (*to herself*): Oh, I could not stand it…could not.

INDU: Stand what, Mother? What do you mean? You could not stand me? You thought I was in your way? I was always in your way, wasn't I?

MRS. VIRK: You were never in my way. You and him…

INDU: Him? Mother, say it—"Your father." Say it, Mother.

MRS. VIRK: Oh, Daughter, why do you have to be so cruel?

INDU: Am I being cruel? You just told me I was not a good daughter—the kind of daughter you wanted me to be. And I am the one being cruel?

MRS. VIRK: How can you twist my words? Just like him. Just like him—sitting there with books, with newspapers…passing judgments.

INDU: Mother, he never spoke a harsh word to you, for that matter, not to anyone else.

MRS. VIRK: Oh, he never said anything to me, but not saying anything sometimes is as bad as saying something horrible. Oh, he never said anything to me—just looked and watched.

INDU: You were busy, Mother, managing the house, your parties, and your friends. You were never home.

MRS. VIRK: I was a good wife and a good mother. He never complained, not even for one day. And look at you—both of you turned out to be fine young ladies. I can't change your luck. No parent can. You don't know how it hurts me to see you like this. I did my best. God is my witness. Like any mother, I wish I could make your luck. You don't know how it hurts. (*Sniffling*.)

INDU: Mother, you don't have to worry about me.

MRS. VIRK: How can you say that? You are my daughter, too.

(*Doorbell rings*.)

INDU: Here comes your daughter!

MRS. VIRK: Who?

INDU: Sonu.

MRS. VIRK: How do you know?

INDU (*pointing toward the keys on the table*): The keys.

(*Mrs. Virk collects herself and rushes to open the door. She disappears in the hallway. Sonu rushes inside bypassing Mrs. Virk and looks around. Indu holds the keys. Sonu takes the keys and hurries outside.*)

SONU (*to Mrs. Virk*): I forgot the keys. I didn't want to wake you up at night.

(*Mrs. Virk is standing near the hallway watching Sonu. Indu does not look up from the book.*)

MRS. VIRK: How late?

SONU (*agitated*): I don't know. I don't want to wake you up.

MRS. VIRK: You think I will be sleeping?

SONU: Don't worry, Mother. I am with friends. Bye.

(*Sonu disappears in the hallway. Mrs. Virk is looking in that direction. The door closes behind Sonu. Slowly, Mrs. Virk returns to her seat and resumes knitting.*)

INDU (*without looking up*): I have asked the store manager to give me extra hours of work on weekends.

MRS. VIRK: More work!

SCENE TWO

INDU: There is not much to be done around here, and we can use extra money. The car needs repairs. I also want to enroll in one or two classes.

MRS. VIRK: Classes!

INDU: I want to get a diploma.

MRS. VIRK: Diploma!

INDU: Something! I do not know, open a store, open a day care, work in a lab. I do not know, something or the other.

MRS. VIRK: I can also work in Lal's restaurant.

INDU: There is no need for you to work there. Besides, what would you do? You can barely keep up with the household work.

MRS. VIRK: You never lifted a finger in your father's house. But here, when you had to, you did. Besides, they offered to help. They seem like God-fearing people. Yes, that is what they are, God fearing. They never skip Sunday service and always make contributions in the temple.

INDU: Mother, it is better to stand on our own two feet. There are plenty of other jobs. As I said, you never worked in the kitchen in your own house; now you want to wash dishes in the restaurant.

Mrs. Virk: You did.

Indu: At that time, I could not think. I did not know what to do and where to look. And...and when Anil and I went to the restaurant, the owner used to be very respectful—

Mrs. Virk: He had better be respectful. Your father saved his father from bankruptcy many times. When the son came here, he borrowed money from your father for his ticket....He'd better be respectful.

Indu (*agitated*): As I said, Mother, there is no need for you to work in his restaurant. I did because I had to. I did not have any experience. (*Pause.*) I had never worked anywhere else. My husband had just passed away. I could not think straight. I had too much on my mind. (*Pause.*) I needed a full-time job to sponsor you.

Mrs. Virk (*troubled*): All alone, all alone. You could have come home.

Indu: How could I? Day in and day out with the thought of Father looking at me and feeling sorry for me. Besides, I thought all of you would come here after his retirement.

Mrs. Virk: Oh, why did you come here? What was the need? There were plenty of young boys with land, jobs, from good families. There was no need for you to come here.

INDU: Oh, I don't know, Mother. You should have discussed that with Father. Did you have somebody in mind, Mother?

MRS. VIRK: Yes, I did. There were a few who were begging for your hand, but your father did not listen to me. He was so adamant to send you here.

INDU: Did you tell Father that you wanted me to settle down near you? Did you tell Father that you could not bear the thought of me going far away from you? Did you, Mother?

MRS. VIRK (*agitated*): Yes, yes.

INDU: Father always listened to you. Did you try to convince him, Mother, that you loved me so much, you could not live with the thought of your firstborn settling down so far away?

MRS. VIRK (*hesitantly*): Yes, I did. I did. I did many times.

INDU: But, Mother, did you plead my case to him, not to send me so far away, plead my case as you used to do for Sonu when she wanted to stay over with her friends or you wanted her to accompany you on school days? Did you, Mother? Did you plead my case, Mother?

MRS. VIRK: I did. You could have had servants, a beautiful home with a garden, and comfortable life.

INDU: But, Mother, did you beg Father not to send me far away?

MRS. VIRK (*sniffles*): God is my witness, I did.

INDU: I think, I think deep down in your heart, you were pleased that I would go far away. Weren't you Mother?

MRS. VIRK (*sniffles*): Oh, you are so cruel!

INDU: Do not worry, Mother. Your secret is safe with me. Both of you wanted me out of there.

MRS. VIRK (*surprised*): Both?

INDU: Of course, both—you and Father!

MRS. VIRK: What do you mean?

INDU: You wanted me out of there because I was like a useless extra limb hanging around your body...an extra burden. I did not fit in your scheme of things... your lifestyle. And Father, he wanted me out because he thought I should stay away; I should settle far away from both of you, mother and daughter...two peas in a pod as they say here.

MRS. VIRK: Why? What did we do to you?

INDU: I do not know, Mother. What do you think?

SCENE TWO

MRS. VIRK: Did your father discuss that with you?

INDU: Discuss what?

MRS. VIRK: His wish.

INDU: No, not in so many words.

MRS. VIRK: What did he say?

INDU: It does not matter now, Mother. How does it matter now? It does not matter at all!

(*Indu gets up and begins to put away the magazines and books and to straighten out the cushions, etc. Abruptly, she turns toward Mrs. Virk.*)

INDU: But look at us! Look at us, Mother. Here we are. Here we are—you and me. My dear father, I wonder what would he say if he were alive?

MRS. VIRK: If he were alive, I would not be sitting here. I would be in my own home.

INDU: Mother, you can always go back to your home.

MRS. VIRK: Both of you are here.

INDU: Both of you can go back, Mother. I filed the papers when Father was alive. I did not want you to feel that after him, I would back down, so I let the process go through. You could have told me that you wanted to stay behind. It would have saved both of us a lot of heartache.

Mrs. Virk: Who is there for me now?

Indu: You and Sonu.

Mrs. Virk: Sonu has a mind of her own. She couldn't care less if anyone lives or dies. She surely has a mind of her own. She won't listen. She is not like you.

Indu: How do you know? How do you know that I don't have a mind of my own? I do, Mother. I do, but I choose to do others' biddings, fool that I am.

Mrs. Virk (*ignoring Indu*): She has a mind of her own.

Indu: What do you know about me? Do you think I want to work in a store for the rest of my life? She refuses to lift a finger. At least she should carry her own weight.

Mrs. Virk: I have asked her many times to find work. And I have offered to work in the Tikki restaurant. You are also being stubborn.

Indu: You love her, Mother. She always was your favorite, your companion on your trips to the mall, your little confidante when you were angry at Father

SCENE TWO

and me, your little doll to parade among your friends as your cherished accomplishment.

MRS. VIRK: I love you both.

INDU (*to herself*): Some imprints are too deep to be erased; no time can fill them.

MRS. VIRK: I love you both.

INDU: Maybe.

MRS. VIRK: How can you doubt my love for you?

INDU: You love her as a mother loves her child.

MRS. VIRK: How so?

INDU: With devotion, protection, and adoration.

MRS. VIRK: You and your father go into these reveries that only you can understand.

INDU: Mother, he is dead.

MRS. VIRK: You are my firstborn. How could I not love you?

INDU: You told me yourself the day I was born—I took him away from you. You said it yourself.

MRS. VIRK: Oh, you and—

INDU: And my father. Yes, Mother. Good night, Mother!

(*Indu goes upstairs without waiting for Mrs. Virk's reply.*)

MRS. VIRK (*whispers to herself*): Good night. Oh, God forgive me. Time is spinning backward. Forgive me.

(*Indu is halfway up the stairs before suddenly returning to the living room.*)

INDU (*raising her voice*): And let me tell you once and for all, I do not want to hear the name of Tikki restaurant here. Do you hear me, Mother? Do not mention him or his family's name in my house.

Mrs. Virk is taken aback. She begins to sort out the yarn in the basket. Indu hurriedly goes upstairs.

Curtain.

SCENE THREE

Same Saturday. Late evening. Mrs. Virk is knitting. She is facing the muted television. All other lights are off. Indu comes downstairs. She turns on the light.

INDU: Sonu is not home yet?

MRS. VIRK (*without looking up*): No.

INDU: I heard voices. I thought she was home.

MRS. VIRK (*hesitantly*): It was Lal and his wife.

INDU: This late? (*Pause.*) What do they want?

MRS. VIRK: They invited us for dinner. And discussed the job offer.

INDU: He doesn't want to give up, does he?

MRS. VIRK: He is just offering a helping hand.

INDU (*agitated*): We are doing just fine without his helping hand.

MRS. VIRK: I don't understand—

INDU (*loudly*): What is there to understand, Mother?

MRS. VIRK (*taken aback, calmly*): He brought it up himself. I did not ask him. And...and there is no shame in working there. It is just for a few months. He even mentioned that Sonu can also work there for a few hours per day.

INDU: I said no and that is it.

MRS. VIRK: I do not know why you have to be so hard-headed about this. He is offering to help. It is not that I have been begging him.

INDU: Why do you want to wash dishes? And Sonu, why would she want to serve other people? You never did that sort of thing your entire life. I am begging you again and again to stop this obsession.

MRS. VIRK: You are the one being so obstinate about it.

INDU (*agitated*): I do not want to discuss it anymore. Let us leave it.

MRS. VIRK (*annoyed*): No discussion! No discussion like a reasonable person. No discussion!

INDU: Yes, no discussion. Not on this topic.

MRS. VIRK: This is what normal people do. People discuss with each other, but you want to draw the line that no one is supposed to cross. If one does, God forbid—

INDU: I said no. And when do I ever ask you for anything?

MRS. VIRK: I just want to help.

INDU: If you really want to help, then you can come with me and work for a few hours where I work.

MRS. VIRK: I don't know anything about working in a store.

INDU: There are women working there who do not speak much English.

MRS. VIRK: Speaking English is not the problem.

INDU: Then, what?

MRS. VIRK: Working with strange people...I—

INDU: It is easier than you think: put in your hours and come home.

MRS. VIRK: That family owes us that much. For generations, we have helped them out. This is the least they can do for us.

INDU (*angrily*): I do not care about the debt owed to our past generations by him or his ancestors. I do not care about that. I have said it many times before, and I am saying it again, Mother, I do not want you or Sonu to work there.

Mrs. Virk: Oh, Daughter, I just want to help.

Indu: There is another way to help me if you really want to help.

Mrs. Virk: Just like that. Whatever you say, right?

Indu: I have my reasons.

Mrs. Virk: You worked there, didn't you?

Indu: Didn't I tell you, at that time, it seemed like I had no choice. (*To herself*) I was numb, frozen inside and outside, complete whiteness just like.... (*Collecting herself*) Oh, why do you have to keep on hammering this like a nail in my heart? Stop it, Mother.

Mrs. Virk: I do not see the harm in it. A few more dollars coming in, I just want to help. (*Sniffles*.)

Indu: There are other ways to make a dollar. I do not want to argue with you anymore. (*Indu walks away*.)

Mrs. Virk: Walk away! Just like him.

Indu: You sucked the life out of him. I will be dammed if I let you do the same to me.

SCENE THREE

MRS. VIRK: What a cruel thing to say!

INDU: Were you at home when he passed away? Were you nursing him, Mother? Sonu told me that when he passed away, you were not at home. Is she right, Mother? Let us discuss. You want to discuss? Let us discuss. He was bedridden for the last five months of his life. Why didn't you tell me? I could have taken care of him. You say discuss. There is plenty to discuss. Let us discuss.

MRS. VIRK (*sniffles*): We did not want to worry you. (*Pause.*) He didn't want to worry you.

INDU: You didn't want me there. Isn't that the truth? Oh, let us discuss. You relish thrashing out everything, don't you, Mother?

(*Indu sits beside Mrs. Virk, not too close, at an angle so that she can see her face. Mrs. Virk hesitates and tries to move her torso away.*)

INDU: Here it is. Hold your breath, Mother. Here comes the discussion. After Anil's death, both husband and wife came to my house and offered me work. After a month or so, I started to work, in the beginning a few hours, slowly it was maximum fifty to sixty hours per week. It was good. I didn't mind. I came home tired, had a good night's sleep. After a few months, I needed a letter stating how much I was making and how long I had been working.

Mrs. Virk: A job letter. For what?

Indu: For your sponsorship. For your immigration.

Mrs. Virk: Oh! And did he refuse to give it?

Indu: No, Mother. He did give me one, but with a price.

Mrs. Virk: Price!

Indu: Yes, Mother, a price!

Mrs. Virk: Price!

Indu: You are a woman. You can understand what kind of price a man can ask a woman to pay. Or do you want to discuss that as well? Do you want me to provide you with the details, Mother? (*Her voice is breaking and she is sobbing.*) Now, tell me, do you want to work in his restaurant? Do you want Sonu to work there?

(*Mrs. Virk leaves her knitting in her lap. She hesitates. Her arms move as if she is going to embrace Indu, but she does not. Instead, she places her hand on Indu's knee to console her.*)

Indu: You want to work in a place where in the darkness...I remember it as if it was yesterday...

(*It is dark on stage. Indu remembers. The light comes on a cashier's counter in the restaurant. Lal is standing behind the counter. The doorbell is heard, indicating someone has just left.*)

LAL (*loudly*): Indu, you can stop now, it is closing time.

(*Indu enters.*)

INDU: I was waiting for the—

LAL: Oh, yes, the letter.

INDU: You said that you will have it today.

LAL (*gently touching her hand*): Why are you always so quiet? Is it Anil? Let me help you forget Anil.

INDU (*hastily removing her hand*): I don't want to forget him.

LAL: How long will you continue like this? You must feel lonely. Let me—

INDU: It is getting late. The letter—

LAL (*agitated*): You think you are above all us mortals. You keep this air of holiness, this aura of respectability, but underneath I know—

INDU: I am no—

LAL: Let me help you. How long will you shut yourself from the world…deny yourself—

INDU: I am not denying myself anything.

LAL (*sarcastically*): Here gentility is nothing but a burden. Money is the real equalizer. And you must—

INDU: Don't you worry about me. Please, let me have the letter.

LAL (*pouring a drink*): At least have a drink with me.

INDU: You know I don't drink.

LAL: In celebration of the letter. (*Pause*.) You have been working in the kitchen for a few months. I think—I think it is time for a promotion.

INDU: Promotion?

LAL: From next week, you can work on the floor, make extra money, tips—

INDU: I am all right in the kitchen.

LAL: Why do you want to waste your time there when—

INDU: I don't mind working in the kitchen.

LAL: Away from people? You are an educated girl, living in an advanced country. You—

INDU: It is getting late.

LAL: Who is waiting for you?

INDU: For you, your wife and children.

LAL: They are not going anywhere.

INDU (*about to leave*): I can get it tomorrow.

LAL: I'd like to, as they say here, get to know you better.

INDU: It is getting late.

LAL: When your family comes, we won't have time.

INDU: Time for what?

LAL: To know each other.

INDU: It is getting late. Please—

(*Lal takes out an envelope from the cash register. He holds it in his hand.*)

LAL (*laughing*): Here it is. Come and get it.

(*Indu tries to take the envelope from Lal, but he steps back. She tries again, but he steps aside, out of her reach.*)

INDU (*angrily*): You have had too much to drink.

(*Indu is about to leave. Her back is to him. He reaches behind her and stops her by grabbing her arm.*)

LAL: Here, here, take the letter. But first, let us get to know—

INDU (*pushing him away*): Let me go.

LAL: How can I? I have been thinking of you for a long time. I have been asking myself, "When will she need me?"

INDU: I don't need you.

LAL: I need you. I think you need me, too, don't you?

INDU (*pushing him away*): Let me go. (*Loudly*) Please, let me go.

(*Lal is laughing.*)

(*It is dark in the restaurant. The living room area is lighted. Indu is crying, staring at the floor. She has her hands over her ears.*)

MRS. VIRK: I thought he was a God-fearing man.

INDU: When people come here, they leave their God behind.

MRS. VIRK: What a rascal! Heathen! Your father saved his family from bankruptcy more than once. This is how he repaid! Why didn't you tell me before?

INDU (*gets up suddenly*): What for, Mother? You don't have the heart of a mother—not for me. Discuss? She wants to discuss?

(*Indu slowly moves toward the stairs. Mrs. Virk stretches out one of her arms toward her. Indu walks away.*)

MRS. VIRK (*confused*): Ah! (*She resumes her knitting.*)

(*The lights are dimmed and the curtain is drawn as Indu is leaving to go upstairs.*)

SCENE FOUR

It is Sunday morning. Indu is drinking tea and reading. Cups and plates are lying on the dining table. Mrs. Virk comes downstairs.

MRS. VIRK: I am going to the temple. Would you like to come?

INDU (*without looking up from her book*): No, but I will drive you there.

MRS. VIRK: Mrs. Singh is coming. She phoned me this morning.

INDU: What time should I pick you up?

MRS. VIRK: She will give me a ride. Do you want to come?

INDU: Maybe next time.

MRS. VIRK: Afterward, she has invited me to her place.

INDU: If you need a ride, call me.

(*Mrs. Virk rushes with the empty cups and plates to the kitchen. She rushes back and tries to straighten the*

SCENE FOUR

things on the dining table. A car horn is heard. She collects her purse and is about to leave.)

INDU: Aren't you going to invite them inside?

MRS. VIRK (*anxious and in a hurry*): We will be late. (*Looking at Indu*) She said it will only waste time coming in and going out. She said that she will come inside some other time.

(*Without waiting for Indu's reply, Mrs. Virk leaves in a hurry and disappears in the hallway. Indu does not move her eyes from the reading material. Sonu comes down the stairs in night clothes.*)

SONU: What was that commotion about? It is impossible to sleep around here.

INDU: It was Mother.

SONU: Where is she?

INDU: She went to the temple.

SONU: So early!

(*Sonu goes to the kitchen and returns with a mug in her hand. She sips tea. She climbs on the sofa chair and folds her legs.*)

INDU: How was the movie?

SONU: It was interesting.

INDU: When did you come in?

SONU: I don't know. It was pretty late.

INDU: What are your plans for today?

SONU: I don't know.

INDU: Do you want to come to the store with me?

SONU: I don't know. I feel very tired.

INDU: We can go to the mall and later do the groceries.

SONU: I want to sleep in.

(*Pause.*)

INDU: Sonu, I don't want to rush you, but—but you should try to find a part-time job.

SONU: Job? Where?

INDU: I can ask for a few hours for you where I work.

SONU: I am so tired.

SCENE FOUR

INDU: I want to enroll in some sort of program at the community college. If you want, you can also enroll in one or two classes.

SONU: What program?

INDU: I am not sure yet. What interests you?

SONU (*disinterested*): I do not know. Do I have to know all that right now?

INDU: You must be getting bored at home.

SONU: Not really.

INDU: For now, I will ask for a few hours at my work. They always have an opening. In the meantime, you should start thinking about what you want to do in the future.

SONU: What do you mean?

INDU: What I mean is, these types of jobs are good for a short while; you get the experience, you will get to know the culture, but in the long run, you should get some degree or diploma.

SONU: I do not know what I want to do. (*With irritation*) Do I have to decide all that now? Can't it wait?

INDU: Take your time. Look around. We can go to the community college tomorrow and look at the options.

SONU: Can't it wait?

INDU: It is not like back home—

SONU: You want money!

INDU (*raising her voice*): No, I don't want money.

SONU: Then, why do you talk about work all the time?

INDU: It is time you start sharing some responsibilities around here.

SONU: I was all right back home.

INDU: You can always go back.

(*Pause.*)

SONU: Mother said she is asking around for work for herself.

INDU (*agitated*): What?

SONU: Yes! That's what she said.

INDU: What would she do?

SCENE FOUR

Sonu: I don't know.

Indu: I have asked her to come with me several times. (*Pause*.) There are quite a few ladies of her age working there.

Sonu: You know she has her own way of doing things.

Indu: For now, I make enough money for all of us. Starting next month, I will be working on weekends, and I have changed working hours to afternoon shift during weekdays as well. We can both take classes.

Sonu: I thought you were already working on weekends.

Indu: I fill in only if someone is absent.

Sonu: I don't know. Classes! I am sick of classes. You don't need a diploma or a degree to work in a store, do you?

Indu: But why do you want to work in a store forever unless you own one yourself? Even then, you should learn something about accounting and management.

(*Silence*.)

Indu: Who did you go out with last night?

Sonu: Rani and her cousin.

INDU: Ajit?

SONU (*as if waking up*): Do you know him?

INDU: Anil and I used to do our groceries at his parents' store.

SONU: So you do know him!

INDU: Anil knew him. I have met him a few times.

SONU: What do you think?

INDU: About what?

SONU: About Ajit.

INDU: As I said, I have met him only a few times. I do not know much about him. He seems like a nice young man.

SONU: Doesn't Mother go to temple with his mother?

INDU: Mrs. Singh?

SONU: Do you know her?

INDU: As much as I know her son. When Mr. Singh passed way, we went to his funeral. That's about it. But I do see her in the store from time to time. Ask Mother. They seem to be spending a lot of time together.

SCENE FOUR

SONU: He says he owns two stores.

INDU: His parents own two stores. They came here more than twenty years ago and worked really hard to buy these stores.

SONU: He does not have any diploma.

INDU: He has been getting on the job training all his life. What does that have to do with us?

SONU: You don't need a diploma to work in a store.

INDU: That is what you want to do for the rest of your life—work in a store!

SONU: I don't know.

INDU: You are young. Take one or two years to find your way. Do not rush into anything. Mother sometimes—sometimes she gets carried away. But you have a chance to be what you want to be. Don't let this opportunity slip away!

SONU (*disinterested in what Indu is saying*): When is Mother coming back?

INDU: I guess late in the evening.

SONU: So she is back to her usual wanderings.

INDU: What do you mean?

SONU: She is doing what she does best.

INDU: What is that?

SONU: Staying out of the house.

INDU: She just went to the temple. (*Pause.*) I can make breakfast for us.

SONU: Not right now. I don't feel so good.

INDU: You do not get enough sleep. You stay up too late. Did you eat anything last night?

SONU: Chips.

INDU: Chips!

SONU (*uneasy*): And pop.

INDU (*putting away reading materials*): What you need is a good breakfast!

SONU: I feel so tired. My body is aching. I want to lie down, maybe sleep for a while.

INDU: You can sleep here. (*She straightens out cushions on the sofa.*) In the meantime, I will do the groceries.

SONU: I would rather sleep in my bed.

INDU (*feels Sonu's forehead*): You do not look so good. You are a bit warm. Let me bring toast and tea. Eat something first and then sleep.

SONU: No, I don't want anything.

(*Sonu walks toward the stairs. She is unsteady and disoriented. Indu collects cups and plates and takes them to the kitchen. She returns to the living room. She stops at the table behind the sofa and stares at the pictures while repositioning them. She turns around to look at Sonu who is slowly climbing the stairs while holding tightly onto the railing. After a few steps, she falls down. She lands at the bottom of the stairs. Indu rushes to her. She calls out her name. Sonu is unconscious. Indu calls out her name again. She becomes nervous and frantic. She runs to the phone.*)

INDU: Hi, my name is Indu Virk. Our address is—there has been an accident. My sister is unconscious. Please hurry. Sonu! Sonu! Wake up, Sonu!

(*While on the phone, Indu is watching Sonu lying on the floor. She rushes back to Sonu and kneels beside her, stroking her hair. In the background, an ambulance siren is heard. People are talking, but the conversation is unclear. Slowly, the lights are dimmed and the curtain is drawn.*)

SCENE FIVE

The following Sunday. Late morning.

Sonu is lying on the sofa, covered with a blanket. The television is on, but it is on mute. Its glare is seen in the living room. Indu is sitting on the sofa armchair, stroking Sonu's hair. There is a teapot, cups, cookies, etc., on the dining table.

INDU: How are you feeling?

SONU: All right.

INDU: Tomorrow is your follow-up. I will drive you to the doctor.

SONU: In the morning?

INDU: In the late afternoon.

SONU: Where is Mother?

INDU: She went to the temple with Mrs. Singh.

SONU: It seems every Sunday, she…

INDU: She stays busy. It is good for her.

Sonu: Did you tell her?

Indu: No.

Sonu: I thought you did.

Indu: It is not my place. In the hospital, I requested the staff not to mention the real reason for your being there to our mother. She thinks you tripped and fell. She thinks you have a concussion.

Sonu: Oh.

Indu: Are you going to tell her?

Sonu: What for?

Indu: She is your mother. Don't you think she needs to know?

Sonu: If you want to tell her, go ahead.

Indu: It is not my place to tell. How can you be so unfeeling about it?

Sonu: I didn't know myself.

Indu: What?

Sonu: I swear. I was not aware.

(*Silence.*)

Sonu: Was it a boy or a girl?

Indu: I did not ask.

Sonu: Maybe it was too early to tell.

Indu: We can call them, in case you want to know.

(*Silence.*)

Sonu: Maybe some other day.

Indu: How are you feeling?

Sonu: I don't know.

Indu: You have to take care of yourself.

Sonu: I am fine.

Indu: You have to be careful. What one does has long-term implications, not only for oneself, but for the child one brings into this world. Not only that, but…

Sonu: You mean family honor!

Indu: Well…

SCENE FIVE

Sonu: Do you think she cares?

Indu: She cares for you. She loves you.

Sonu: The only person she cares for is herself. And it probably would have mattered to him, but he is dead.

Indu: Sometimes you can be so cynical.

Sonu: Where is she? Even if I had a concussion or headache or fever, where is she? When was the last time she sat with us to eat, watch a movie, or have a sensible conversation?

Indu: She does most of the housework.

Sonu: That's the least she can do.

Indu: She does talk and sit around with us.

Sonu: Only when she wants to grumble to you. I don't know how you can take it—nothing new, same old stuff. She goes after you like a hawk. How can you stand it?

Indu: It is not as bad when you are around. You are my shield!

(*Indu gets up and pours tea from the teapot and hands it to Sonu.*)

INDU: Here, get up.

(*Sonu sits up. She takes the mug from Indu. Indu fluffs the pillow and straightens out the blanket. She gives Sonu cookies and places the cookie plate on the table. The atmosphere is pleasant. Sonu is changing channels on the television. Indu pours a cup of tea for herself and returns to the armchair.*)

INDU: She loves you. She adores you. You used to accompany her everywhere. She used to dress you up like a little doll, a princess.

SONU: So that I could make her look good. I was like a new sari, a set of new bangles, a charm added to her dazzling self.

INDU: She always loved you. She brought you with her everywhere.

SONU: To make herself look good.

INDU: You are mistaken.

SONU: The only person she cares for is herself.

INDU: She adores you. Remember one time, she insisted that I give you the gold bangles Grandmother had given me. Mother made me take them off and hand them to you. I was a little hesitant.

SONU: A little hesitant? You did not want to part with them.

INDU: Oh, she insisted. I can still see her stern face and bulging eyes staring at me. Finally, Father signed me to give them to you. And you lost them. I cried and cried. Both of you kept it from Father for a long time. When he found out, he went for a long walk and returned after dark.

SONU: I remember he slept on the veranda that night. He never mentioned the incident.

INDU: I was very angry with you for a long time. You went around your business as if nothing had happened, with a triumphant look on your face. So young and so cruel, I thought.

SONU: I wanted to hurt you.

INDU: Hurt me? Why? What did I ever do to you?

SONU: He loved you. You were always hovering around him—with a breakfast plate, lunch, a glass of water, milk, this or that. I hated you so much.

INDU: Both of you were out and about. He didn't have anyone.

SONU: There were servants to fetch his things. But you were lingering around all the time. Even Mother said so. Nobody could get near him.

INDU: Mother said that?

SONU: When I lost the bangles, he never yelled at me, never asked me what had happened: how did I lose them? Where did I lose them? After all, they meant something to him; they were his mother's. He stared at me, then at Mother, then at me. Oh, I hated that. Then, he got up and walked away; walked away just like that, without uttering a single word.

(*Pause*.)

INDU: You know he was not much of a talker or yeller. You know that!

SONU: I thought he would say something. Oh, but not him. He walked out. And you followed him. Where did you go? What did he say?

INDU: We walked along the edge of the railway tracks for about an hour. Then, we turned around and came back home. He did not say anything.

SONU: Nothing?

INDU: Nothing.

SONU: I wish he had said something to me. As Mother is always saying, it is better to say something than nothing.

SCENE FIVE

INDU: If one does not understand without words, then lengthy speech will only open the doors for argument, defensiveness, and more words.

SONU: You have very strange views...strange...about everyday, normal things.

INDU: Mother would have reprimanded him that he was making a big fuss for two bangles. She would have taken two of her bangles and given them to me; or rather, she would have thrown them at me or at him.

SONU (*as if talking to herself*): I just wanted him to say something to me. It is better to say something than nothing. (*Pause.*) Would you get the wooden box from the bookcase shelf?

(*Sonu points toward the box. Indu fetches the box and hands it to Sonu. Sonu straightens herself and dusts off the box. She empties the contents onto the coffee table. She turns the box upside down and struggles to open the secret compartment at the bottom of the box. After tinkering, she opens the hidden slot. She takes out a small package wrapped in a piece of cloth and hands it over to Indu.*)

SONU: Here.

INDU (*with excitement*): What is it? (*She unwraps the contents and is surprised and excited to see the con-*

tents.) Oh, my God! The bangles! You didn't lose them after all. (*She slips them onto her wrist.*)

Sonu: I am not that stupid. How could I lose them! Remember, I had to use soap to slip them on.

Indu: Then, why?

Sonu: Oh, I wanted to hurt you and hurt him. I don't know. It seemed so right at that time. It seems so childish now. I just wanted to infuriate him, make him lose his temper.

(*Indu takes off the bangles and returns them to Sonu.*)

Sonu: No, no, you keep them. They are yours.

Indu: Are you sure? (*She slips the bangles back on her wrist. Affectionately*) You little schemer!

(*Silence.*)

Indu: Did you ever hear him say anything to me?

Sonu: No!

Indu: It was not his nature.

Sonu: When you left home, I was so happy.

Indu: Oh, were you?

SONU: I wasn't happy for you, but for me. I thought that finally I will be his little girl, and do all the little things you used to do for him. He will show the newspaper articles to me, ask me to read them—the important ones, the interesting ones—the way you used to do.

INDU: I am glad you had the chance.

SONU: Chance? What chance? He stopped the newspaper subscription and started going to the library to read the newspapers. He brought all his paraphernalia and covered the table near his chair, so nobody had to fetch anything for him. It was as if you took him away with you. There was nothing left for me. (*Sobbing*.)

INDU: Sorry, I am so sorry. Come. Come now. (*She wraps her arm around Sonu's shoulders and wipes her tears*.) You should not get upset in your weak condition. You need to rest. It is so easy to slip into this reverie, but it's no use now. (*Consoling her*) Here, here. You need to rest.

You seemed so happy, always so cheerful and carefree. You and Mother, always on the move—going shopping, to the movies, visiting friends, joking, discussing fashion, festivals...I wanted to be part of you, happy and cheerful, laughing out loudly. I wanted to go out with you and mother. But, whenever I entered the room, I felt like an intruder. Every time I entered the room, the laughter would cease, the conversation would stop.

I would step back and return to sit beside him amid the sea of silence. Oh, how desperately I longed to be part of that laughter. (*Moving her arm away from Sonu*) It seems like all that happened yesterday!

SONU (*collecting herself*): Mother would say that you would rather stay with Father than come with us.

INDU: She never asked me to come along; she never wanted me to come along. (*As if to herself*) Maybe she used to leave me behind on purpose, so—so that she wouldn't feel guilty leaving him, abandoning him with the heap of books.

(*Pause.*)

INDU: Would you tell Mother?

SONU: What do you think?

INDU: It is your call.

SONU: We both know that her concern won't be what happened to me. Somehow, it will become about her; how unlucky she is, husband is dead, or it is your fault for bringing us here.

INDU: I thought both of you wanted to come here.

SONU: I don't know. I was happy there—going to college, had friends, had a life.

INDU: You can always go back.

SONU: You think so?

(*Silence*.)

INDU: Who was the father? Ajit?

SONU: Yes.

INDU: Are you planning to tell him? Marry him?

SONU (*agitated*): I don't know.

INDU: What were you thinking?

SONU: Thinking?

INDU: Actions have consequences.

SONU: Yes, you mentioned this already—not only for you but for your family as well. Honor of the family! What family? Remember, he is dead, and all that went with him.

INDU (*agitated*): Stop saying that he is dead. He is dead for you. Maybe he was dead for you from the beginning. He was nothing but a figurine in the chess game that both of you were playing. How ignorant I was, or rather, stupid.

SONU: You are neither stupid nor ignorant; you just refuse to see things the way they are.

INDU: Back home, it is different. People know each other for generations. In this type of situation, the families step in; all things get taken care of. People come here from everywhere. Nobody knows their background. You have to be careful who you associate with.

(*Pause*.)

SONU: She will be out every Sunday.

INDU: It is not a bad thing to go to temple.

SONU: If you go there to pray! Have you ever seen her praying at home? Give her a few months. She will have a schedule for every day. These walls are too confining for her. You will see.

INDU: Don't be so cynical!

SONU: Remember, I am the one who spent the most time with her. I know her.

INDU: You seem to know everyone.

SONU: So it seems. It is true. I see things as they are, not as they ought to be or can be, with sheer willpower. I see things just the way they are.

INDU: If you are so smart, why did you create this mess for yourself?

SCENE FIVE

SONU: You are in a bigger mess with Mother than you can see. Just as he was.

INDU: I am not in a mess with her or with you.

SONU: That is what you think.

INDU: You have too much imagination. You should start college and make use of this fertile brain of yours. Let me get lunch for you. (*She goes to kitchen.*)

SONU: You don't have to make anything. We will eat leftovers. (*Raises her voice*) I am right about her. You will see.

(*Sonu gets up slowly and folds the blanket. She refills the wooden box with the items she had taken out of it. With an effort, she walks to put the box away on the bookshelf. The clatter of plates can be heard in the background. Sonu returns to the sofa and sits down. She organizes the coffee table. Indu returns with a tray and sets it on the coffee table.*)

SONU: Biryani!

INDU: I made it this morning.

SONU: Thanks!

INDU: Here, take yogurt. You must eat healthy. You need your strength back.

(Their conversation fades away into the background. They eat lunch. Indu brings the fruit tray from the dining table. The lights dim. Slowly, the curtain is drawn.)

SCENE SIX

Same Sunday evening.

Sonu is flipping through reading materials. Indu is sitting at the dining table. She is going through the mail.

SONU: Mother is not home yet?

INDU: I am not sure. Last night, she was saying something about going with Mrs. Singh. (*Looking at the letter with excitement*) I have been accepted.

SONU: Accepted?

INDU (*with excitement*): Accepted in the college.

SONU: College?

INDU: At St. Mary's.

SONU: I did not know you were trying.

INDU: You did not?

(*Pause.*)

SONU: It is out of town, isn't it?

INDU: Yes, about a two-hour drive.

SONU: Two hours?

INDU: Oh, I will move there.

SONU: Move there?

INDU: Yes.

(*Indu continues to go through the mail and other papers.*)

(*Silence.*)

SONU: Ajit came to see me yesterday.

INDU: Yes.

SONU: He said he can't face you. He said he wants to do the right thing.

INDU: And what is that?

SONU: He wants to marry me.

INDU (*with excitement, rushes to hug Sonu*): Congratulations. I am happy for you. (*Returning to the dining table*) But I don't know how I came to figure in this situation.

SONU: Didn't I mention he thinks very highly of you?

INDU: I barely know him; it was Anil. Besides, he should not make such a big commitment because of me.

SONU: Does it matter why he wants to make this commitment as long as he does make the commitment?

INDU: As I mentioned earlier, I barely know him. Moreover, it is between the two of you.

SONU: How strange! Not only does he speak very highly of you, but he also said that he used to come here.

INDU (*agitated*): As I mentioned earlier, he did come here to see my husband. Anil used to help him with his studies.

(*Pause.*)

INDU: Do you care about him?

SONU: I think I do.

INDU: You should not marry him for the wrong reasons.

SONU: Oh no, not for wrong reasons. I am marrying him for all the right reasons. But they may be different from what you think are the right reasons.

INDU: Right is right. It is not a question of what is right for you or what is right for someone else.

Sonu: I disagree. Some things are right for me, or I think they are right for me. They may not be right for you, though.

(*Silence.*)

Sonu: He is the type of person Father would have liked.

Indu: Father? How convenient to remember him!

Sonu: He was my father, too! I know his likes and dislikes.

Indu: I am happy for you.

Sonu: Yes, that's what I thought, that Father would have liked Ajit. He is sincere. Commitment and duty are very high on his list.

(*Pause.*)

Sonu: He said that his mother will discuss the proposal with our mother.

Indu: She is the one who gives her a ride every Sunday.

Sonu: If things work out, would you stay?

Indu: I will be only two hours away. Of course, I will attend my baby sister's wedding.

SCENE SIX

SONU: What if it takes place back home?

INDU: Back home? Did he say so?

SONU: Not in so many words.

INDU: Then?

SONU: One day, we were just talking casually. He said in passing that his grandparents on both sides of the family are in poor health. His mom thinks it will make them happy if we go there for the ceremonies.

INDU: Maybe it will be best for Mother as well. She will have more support there. Moreover, all the preparation, clothes, our jewelry, etc., are there.

SONU: You are right. Our Mother is good at that sort of thing.

INDU: In that case, I will try to come. It all depends if I would be able to take time off from whatever I will be doing at that time.

SONU: You will try, won't you? It won't be the same without you.

INDU: Of course.

(*Pause*.)

INDU: You know what I think? Sometimes, I think growing up around Father, staying around him all the time has limited me in many ways, especially in my outlook on life.

SONU: How so?

INDU: For example, the way Mother and you look at things and handle people seems so foreign to me.

SONU: Maybe so.

INDU: I feel like a stranger in my own house.

SONU: I am sorry if we make you feel that way.

INDU: No, it's not your fault. It's mine.

(*Pause.*)

INDU: Sometimes I think the whole world has passed me by. The whole way of thinking and of doing things…I am stuck in some realm with so much weight on me, unable to move.

SONU: You should be responsible for your life and your life only. The rest is nothing but a mirage.

INDU: My baby sister is so wise.

SONU: You take life too seriously. Do not plan it; let it happen.

INDU: Oh yes, let it happen and happen it will.

SONU: You don't see me worrying.

(*Pause.*)

SONU: Most of the time, things take care of themselves.

INDU (*with a subdued smile*): They do, don't they?

(*Silence.*)

INDU: I have been nothing but a fool. And a fool deserves no luck.

SONU: But Indu, a fool—not that I am saying you are a fool—a fool deserves luck, more than anyone else.

INDU (*smiling*): How so?

SONU: A fool needs luck—more luck than anyone else—to compensate for the foolery of not only of oneself but of the world around as well.

INDU: But does this fool deserve luck?

SONU: Of course. Everyone can use some luck. But first, one should stop being a fool, because if one continues to be a fool, what will more luck do?

INDU: Deserve or not, this fool can use some luck.

Sonu: Well, then—

Indu: Stop being a fool?

Sonu: Precisely.

Indu: I never thought of it that way.

Sonu: Not only must you think, but think ahead, before anyone—

Indu: So what are you thinking now?

Sonu (*thoughtfully*): I—I am thinking that when I go back home, I want to sell my share of the property.

Indu: We must do right by our mother.

Sonu: Otherwise what? He wouldn't like it! You have to wake up. I say time and time again, he is dead.

Indu: Well, not for his sake. She is our mother. Despite her bravado, she will need assistance as she gets older.

Sonu: She does not need anyone now; she would not need anyone then. But when that time comes, we will see.

Indu: I think Mother has the right to its income during her lifetime.

SONU: What does she need it for when she is living here?

INDU: She may want to live there from time to time. But that is not the point. Father willed it that way, and we should honor his wishes.

SONU: He is dead. Moreover, have you seen the will?

INDU (*agitated*): No, no, I have not seen the will.

SONU: Maybe he willed the land that way. He could not have done both. What does she need the income from the house and land for?

INDU: She needs a place to stay when she goes there. What is the rush? Eventually, it will be ours. I do not want to sell my share as long as she is alive.

SONU: I may want to use my share here. If you are so concerned about her, you can buy my share and keep it until she dies.

INDU: You know I do not have that kind of money. Did you talk to Mother about your intentions?

SONU: After the marriage. I do not want to rattle her now.

INDU: So you want her to spend as much as she can on you now, without hesitation. Only then, surprise, surprise! I never saw that coming.

Sonu: You refuse to see. You just want to see what you want to see.

Indu: I always thought both of you were very close.

Sonu: We are. That's why I know her so well.

Indu: That is why you want her to suffer in her old age.

Sonu: Suffer? Suffer, she will not.

(*Pause.*)

Sonu: She has plenty to live on. She is fairly young. She can work.

Indu: Working five to ten hours to stay busy is one thing, but to work for a living is another. She has never worked in her life.

Sonu: Didn't you hear her? She used to teach!

Indu: Teaching youngsters there and working here are not the same. But since you have not worked a day here yourself, what would you know?

Sonu: I don't intend to work either. When I get married to Ajit, I wouldn't have to work, just manage the store.

SCENE SIX

INDU: His mom is in the store from morning until closing time, seven days a week.

SONU: She does not do anything. It is called *managing*.

INDU: You have figured out everything, haven't you?

SONU: Either you figure it out yourself, or others will figure it out for you.

INDU: I never knew my baby sister is so wise. If you decide to marry Ajit, you won't need the money. You don't have to sell your share of the property right away.

(*Mrs. Virk enters in a hurry, out of breath.*)

MRS. VIRK (*with excitement*): I have good news. No, no. I have great news! God has listened to my prayers.

INDU: Mother, what is it?

(*Ignoring Indu, Mrs. Virk walks over to Sonu and she embraces her. Indu sees it and returns to her mail.*)

MRS. VIRK (*with excitement*): Dear Daughter, God has listened to my prayers. I prayed and prayed. A fatherless girl, woman without a husband, two daughters.... Finally, finally, my daughter, finally my prayers are answered, almighty God—

Sonu (*raising her voice*): Mother!

Mrs. Virk: Mrs. Singh! You know Mrs. Singh and her son Ajit, don't you? She asked for your hand for her son! How lucky you are! How lucky I am! (*Hugs Sonu. She holds Sonu's face in her hands.*) How lucky am I? How lucky are you?

Sonu: What did you say?

Mrs. Virk (*exuberantly*): What did I say? I said yes! What do you think? Of course, I said yes. Yes! Yes! (*She hugs Sonu tightly.*)

Sonu: Oh, Mother, let go of me. I can't breathe.

Curtain.

SCENE SEVEN

The following week. Friday late afternoon.

Mrs. Virk and Sonu are in the living room. Mrs. Virk is knitting and Sonu is flipping through a magazine.

SONU: Do you know that she will be leaving?

MRS. VIRK: Leaving? Who?

SONU: Indu.

MRS. VIRK: Why?

SONU: For studies.

MRS. VIRK: She can study here.

SONU: She is planning to leave.

MRS. VIRK: She cannot leave like that.

SONU: She will. That is her plan.

MRS. VIRK: She will not leave. I will see to it.

SONU: What would you do? Put chains on her ankles?

Mrs. Virk: I will…

(*Indu enters. She has her uniform on. Sonu and Mrs. Virk are surprised to see her.*)

Mrs. Virk: You are home early today!

Sonu: Are you all right?

Indu (*to Sonu*): Yes, I am fine. Mother, the house smells so good.

Mrs. Virk: I made *kadhi* for you. I said to myself, "Indu will come home so tired after a day's work. I will make something special for her."

Indu: Thank you, Mother. (*She hurries upstairs.*)

Sonu: Why do women feel so compelled to make up these stories?

Mrs. Virk: What stories?

Sonu: Mother, I have heard you harping for many days that you have the craving for *kadhi*. So, finally, you made it; you made it for yourself. Here you are telling Indu that you cooked it for her, knowing very well that she does not like it; she has never liked it. You know it, Mother, don't you? Then, why?

Mrs. Virk: Oh, hush, girl.

SONU: There is no need for this charade, Mother. There is no one here that you need to impress. You can boil grass; she will eat it and be thankful for it.

MRS. VIRK: Oh, be quiet, girl. In Father's house, you have brothers, sisters, friends, relatives...you leave everything behind. One day, you wake up in a new house with new people around you, new voices, new expectations. You try to be what they want you to be; learn the new ways overnight and pretend not to miss anything of the previous life. You do not dare to offend anyone by saying something, by not following the family rituals, ways of cooking and eating... (*Her voice is broken and agitated.*) All the time, trying to please everyone—

SONU: It was not that bad for you, Mother.

MRS. VIRK: You are surrounded by strange people, yet you act as if you have known them for centuries. You are being watched; your every word is being weighed. You are on trial!

SONU: But Father did not want you to leave your life. You said it yourself. Besides, you did not have to live with his family, not for long periods. He did not want you to stop teaching. You, yourself, did not pursue it. As far as I can remember, it was just the four of us, and our grandparents used to visit us once in a while.

MRS. VIRK: Only after years, when your father was posted far away.

SONU: You had Father on your side.

MRS. VIRK: Not always. He was not the type to take sides.

SONU: You sound as if raging battles were going on back then. As far as I can remember, you always got along with *Bhua ji*.

MRS. VIRK: God bless her. She was the one who used to put some sense in your father's head. She saved my marriage.

SONU: Mother, your marriage was never in danger. I cannot imagine Father leaving you and us behind. He was not that sort of a man.

MRS. VIRK: Your generation does not know what we had to go through.

SONU: I am sure many had tough times, but not you, Mother.

MRS. VIRK: What do you know?

SONU: What, Mother? You had family properties, servants, a good circle of friends and relatives. Look at us! We have to work for everything and leave one job outside and another is waiting at home. You did not have as difficult a life as you are making us believe. Stop grumbling, Mother.

MRS. VIRK: You have your own way of looking at things. You think you are very wise, you know everything.

SONU: Not everything, Mother, but I know you.

MRS. VIRK: Oh, hush, girl, hush. She is coming.

(*Indu comes downstairs and sits at the dining table without looking at either of them.*)

INDU: Mother, everything looks so delicious. Thank you.

(*Sonu's back is to Indu. She looks at Mrs. Virk and smiles. Both get up and slowly move toward the dining table.*)

INDU: Mother, I have enrolled in classes at St. Mary's College.

MRS. VIRK: Isn't it where Anil's sister lives?

INDU: Yes.

MRS. VIRK: It is a long way from here.

INDU: I will be moving there.

MRS. VIRK: Move there?

INDU: Yes, it is only for two years. I think it will be best for all of us.

Mrs. Virk: Two years is a long time.

Indu: If you and Sonu want, you can take over some of my hours in the store.

Mrs. Virk: I will.

Indu: Both of you can come with me tomorrow. I will show you around and introduce you to the supervisor. (*Pause*.) I also want to know what arrangements have been made for the property back home.

Mrs. Virk: It is in your names, yours and Sonu's. Your father arranged it so that during my lifetime, I will use the incomes. And of course, I also receive your father's pension.

Sonu: Farm, and the house, too.

Mrs. Virk: A portion of the house is rented out.

Indu: You can arrange to exchange the money. There are plenty of people who send money back home for their families.

Sonu: But for now, what will we—

Indu: I will take care of the house bills. The other expenses may come to five or six hundred dollars per month. Both of you can manage that much, can't you?

(*Pause.*)

INDU: After a few months, I would like to sell this house. Mother, you may want to return home.

MRS. VIRK: When are you leaving for college?

INDU: Next month.

MRS. VIRK: Next month? So soon!

INDU: What?

MRS. VIRK: Everything seems so right now.

INDU: For me, it is a good time to get something done.

MRS. VIRK: Will you come back to see me?

INDU: Yes, Mother. I am not leaving the country!

(*The phone rings. Sonu hurriedly picks up the phone.*)

SONU (*to Indu*): It is for me. (*Into the phone*) I will call you from upstairs. (*Hangs up the phone and exits.*)

MRS. VIRK: It is so sudden. Anything I said?

INDU: No.

MRS. VIRK: Then, why so sudden?

INDU: It is not what you say or what you do.

MRS. VIRK: Then, what?

INDU: The other day, I—I....Forget it, Mother. It is no use.

(*Pause.*)

MRS. VIRK: I—I...

INDU: Mother, our relationship is lopsided from the beginning. Only, I did not see it. I am not that smart, Mother. I try to fix it, all my life. God is my witness. But there is no fixing it. It is like threadbare soft cotton. The frazzled edges are exposed every time one tries to straighten it out by hand. You have to cut it with scissors. We have to sever our ties.

MRS. VIRK: Blood ties cannot be broken. How can you—

INDU: Distance, Mother, the distance, what force can be more blunt than the distance? Distance between us, Mother, there is no sorting out, no mending it, and no straightening it.

MRS. VIRK: I am your mother and nothing can change that.

INDU: We are suffocating each other. This warp and weft of our lives is too entangled. It is no use. I have tried. God is my witness. (*Picks up the yarn out of the bas-*

ket and tries to sort it out, reflectively.) Mother, warp of our lives is like the strings on a fiddle to be played gently using the bow wrapped in tenderness, love, and compassion, of which you know so little. The woof strung around the bow is either too loose or too tight, devoid of gentleness and kindness that nature sows in every woman's heart, of which you know so little.

MRS. VIRK: I have tried to do my best, but—

INDU: Mother, no weaver can weave like you, but underneath your seamless displays, there are either big knots or loose ends. (*Pause*.) Life is never the beautiful tapestry we try to display to others. Sooner or later, the wheel of time will turn up the wrinkles and rumples we try to hide from ourselves and others. It will stretch out and reveal everything; it always does.

MRS. VIRK: I will always be your mother.

INDU: Yes, and I will always be your daughter.

(*Silence*.)

INDU: If you don't like it here, you can go back. Mother, you are free to do as you please. You have plenty to live off for the rest of your life.

MRS. VIRK: It is not mine alone. It is yours as well.

(*Sonu comes downstairs*.)

INDU: I came home early today to take the car to the garage.

SONU: I can come with you if you wait for me while I get ready.

INDU: I don't know how long it will take in the garage. You will be bored. We can go together this evening.

(*As Indu is about to leave*)

SONU: I have plans for this evening.

(*Indu without looking up, picks up her keys and purse, and leaves.*)

MRS. VIRK: What? You have plans for the evening? You should spend time with your sister. She works so hard. It won't hurt you if once in a while you spend time with her. Go to the movies or shopping.

SONU: I don't ask her to work so hard.

MRS. VIRK: Oh, have some sense!

SONU: Oh, Mother!

(*Sonu is annoyed. She goes upstairs. Mrs. Virk picks up her knitting.*)

Curtain.

SCENE EIGHT

Saturday afternoon. Mrs. Virk is ironing clothes. A laundry basket with clothes is lying on the coffee table. The ironed clothes are neatly hanging over the armchair. The television is on. The phone rings. Mrs. Virk hurriedly answers it. As Indu comes downstairs, Mrs. Virk hastily puts the phone down.

INDU: Who was it, Mother?

MRS. VIRK: Nobody.

INDU: I overheard you saying, "not home," but all of us are at home. So who was it?

MRS. VIRK: No one.

INDU (*raising her voice*): Who was it, Mother?

MRS. VIRK: Somebody who knew Anil, his colleague.

INDU: His colleague? His name?

MRS. VIRK: Patrick.

INDU: Patrick? Why didn't you tell me?

(*Silence.*)

INDU: Did he call previously?

MRS. VIRK: He might have.

INDU: Since you arrived, you have never given me any message. You have cut me off from everyone.

MRS. VIRK: They were Anil's friends.

INDU: Mine, too!

MRS. VIRK: I did not know you want to talk to him.

(*Indu is searching for the phone notebook in the drawer of the desk behind the sofa.*)

INDU: Where is the notebook? It was always here.

(*She walks over to the bookcase and frantically searches for the notebook. When Indu is not looking, Mrs. Virk pulls the notebook out of her purse and hurriedly places it under the pile of books on the table behind the sofa.*)

MRS. VIRK: Here it is! Here is the notebook.

(*Indu swiftly walks over and locates the number. She places the call, but there is no answer. Indu is about to return the notebook to the desk drawer, but hesitates for a minute, and instead, she stores it in her purse. Mrs. Virk is watching her every move.*)

INDU: We can start a new notebook. This belongs to Anil and me.

(*Without waiting for an answer, Indu walks toward the stairs. After a few steps, she returns and looks at Mrs. Virk in silence, and then grabs her purse. Mrs. Virk watches her as Indu leaves to go upstairs without saying a word. As Sonu comes downstairs, Indu hurriedly bypasses her without saying a word.*)

SONU: What is wrong with her?

MRS. VIRK: Nothing.

(*Mrs. Virk exits with the ironing board and iron in the hallway. She returns and exits with the laundry basket. She returns hastily.*)

SONU: What did you say to her now?

MRS. VIRK: Nothing. (*Pointing to the hanging clothes*) I ironed your clothes.

SONU: Mother!

MRS. VIRK: Phone call—I forgot to tell her.

SONU: Forgot? Or you chose not to tell?

MRS. VIRK: Oh, hush!

Sonu: One day, you will get caught in your own web.

Mrs. Virk: Web?

Sonu: Your own entangled web, Mother. (*She picks up her ironed clothes and goes upstairs.*)

(*Indu comes downstairs and fetches the ironing board, iron, and laundry basket. She sets the ironing board in front of the television and begins to iron her clothes.*)

Mrs. Virk: Here, you want me to iron your clothes?

Indu: Did you ask for Sonu's permission to iron her clothes?

Mrs. Virk (*hesitantly*): I—I...

Indu (*raising her voice*): Did you?

(*Mrs. Virk walks away. Sonu returns downstairs all dressed up.*)

(*Silence.*)

(*Car horn is heard in the background.*)

Mrs. Virk (*to Indu*): Do you want to come?

Indu: Come? Where?

Mrs. Virk: Mrs. Singh has invited all of us.

Indu: And you are telling me now?

Mrs. Virk: We will wait.

Indu: If you wanted me to come with you, you would have told me earlier to get ready.

Mrs. Virk: We will wait.

Indu: Wait?

Sonu (*to Indu*): Didn't you know?

(*Sonu and Indu look at Mrs. Virk.*)

(*Another car horn is heard.*)

Mrs. Virk (*hesitantly*): I—I…it slipped my mind.

Indu (*to Sonu*): Don't make them wait.

(*Sonu hesitates. She looks at Mrs. Virk for a moment. Then both of them exit.*)

(*Indu leaves the ironing and sits down. She gets up and moves the ironing board away from the television. She sits down again. After a while, she gets up and moves around. She picks up a cup from the kitchen counter and throws it at the wall. She looks at the picture of her father.*)

INDU: Stop staring at me. (*Raising her voice*) You think I am a fool, don't you? (*She picks up the picture and throws it on the sofa.*) Stop it. Stop looking at me. Stop staring. Why does everyone have to die on me? (*Pause.*) What am I doing here? Is just being alive enough? Keeping up with the promise to breathe, that is all. Nothing before it; may be nothing after it. All this fuss for nothing. (*She returns to the sofa and picks up the picture. She curls up on the sofa. Looking upward*) Cradle my heart in the hammock of faith…I want to rest, touching the branches of the heavens… never to wake up again. Let me disappear. Let me float away, veiled in the layers of soft clouds. Take me away. You must take me away.

(*Slowly the lights dim. Curtain.*)

SCENE NINE

A few days later. A teapot, cups, and plates are lying on the dining table and coffee table. Sonu is reading a magazine. She is sitting in the armchair with her back toward the stairs so that she can see Mrs. Virk. Mrs. Virk enters from the kitchen with an elastic bandage. She sits on sofa and places her foot on the tea table and begins to wrap her ankle.

Indu is in the middle of the stairs. As she hears the conversation, she suddenly stops and steps back to listen.

SONU: You are not planning to break your ankle, Mother, are you?

MRS. VIRK: I don't know what you are talking about.

SONU: You know very well, Mother, what I am talking about!

MRS. VIRK: Hush, girl!

SONU: It is over, Mother. It won't work this time, not anymore.

MRS. VIRK: Hush, girl. You must hush.

Sonu: She does not have much to lose. She lost her husband and she has lost her father. She does not have much to lose, Mother.

Mrs. Virk: Hush, girl. Oh, hush! You must stop.

Sonu: Do not push it, Mother!

Mrs. Virk: You don't know anything.

Sonu: I know plenty, Mother. She is not Father, not your husband. She is your daughter. At this point, she has nothing to lose. She can leave and never come back.

Mrs. Virk (*nervously, as if to herself*): She can't do that.

(*Pause.*)

Mrs. Virk (*to Sonu*): Can she? (*Pause.*) Would she?

(*Pause.*)

Mrs. Virk (*to herself*): No! No!

(*Pause.*)

Mrs. Virk (*suddenly turns to Sonu*): Can she?

(*Sonu nods in affirmation.*)

MRS. VIRK: But she will not. She will not.

SONU: What is holding her here? Your love?

MRS. VIRK: She cannot leave just like this. She simply cannot. I will not let her. I simply will not.

SONU: Mother, let it go.

MRS. VIRK: You will see. I will not let it happen.

SONU: What are you thinking now, Mother?

(*While Mrs. Virk turns to hoist her wrapped ankle on a cushion on the sofa, she sees Indu, who starts to come down the stairs.*)

INDU: Well, Mother, it is time for me to leave. (*With concern*) What happened?

MRS. VIRK (*sniffles*): Oh, nothing.

INDU: What happened, Mother?

MRS. VIRK: Oh, nothing you should worry yourself about.

INDU: Is it hurting?

(*Indu tries to examine the ankle, but Mrs. Virk would not let her touch it.*)

Mrs. Virk: Don't you worry. It hurts a little, but it is nothing.

Indu: What happened?

Mrs. Virk: Last night, I tripped and fell in the bedroom. It is nothing. I think I just twisted the ankle, nothing serious. (*Sniffles*.)

Indu: Why didn't you wake me up?

Mrs. Virk: I did not want to bother you. (*Sniffles*.) I didn't want you to worry. Today, you have a long drive ahead of you.

Indu: Mother, I cannot leave you like this. Let us go to the hospital and get it checked.

Mrs. Virk (*a triumphant look toward Sonu*): It is nothing. I will be all right. You must leave on time. You must call me as soon as you reach there.

Indu (*with concern*): Are you sure, Mother?

Mrs. Virk: I made breakfast, and a hot pot of tea is on the stove. I also packed lunch for you to take with you.

Indu: You should not have done all this work in your condition.

(*Indu walks behind the sofa and disappears into the kitchen. Sonu shakes her head while staring at Mrs. Virk. Mrs. Virk takes a deep breath and settles back in her seat. She picks up her knitting. Still chewing food and drinking tea, Indu rushes back from the kitchen.*)

INDU: Would you be able to walk to the car? I can drive it closer to the door.

MRS. VIRK: Why?

INDU: To drive you to the hospital.

MRS. VIRK: No need for that. Just a little sprain.

INDU: Just in case—

MRS. VIRK: I will try.

(*Sonu once again shakes her head.*)

INDU: After your checkup, Mother, if it gets late, you can take a taxi to come home. Otherwise, I will drop you at home. Let me know how you feel. I will inform the workplace accordingly.

MRS. VIRK (*sniffles*): I will be all right. There is no need to go to the hospital.

Indu: For my peace of mind, let us be sure. Let us get it checked.

Mrs. Virk: You will be late.

Indu: I will be fine.

Mrs. Virk: Must you go today?

Indu: Yes. Anil's sister is waiting for me. I have already postponed the trip once.

Mrs. Virk: Will you be all right?

Indu: Yes, Mother. Would you be all right?

Mrs. Virk: I don't have any choice, do I? After your father—

Sonu (*hastily interrupting Mrs. Virk*): Don't you worry, Indu. We will be just fine. She is not leaving the country, Mother. It is only a two-hour drive.

Mrs. Virk: It is my heart, a mother's heart. I worry about you both. Don't blame me for that!

Indu (*giving Mrs. Virk a stern look*): Yes, Mother. For now, let us go and look after your ankle.

(*Sonu looks up from the magazine and shakes her head. Mrs. Virk looks at her with disapproval. She has a faint smile on her face. As soon as Indu turns toward them,*

SCENE NINE

Mrs. Virk's face shows signs of pain. Sonu returns to her reading. Indu goes upstairs.)

MRS. VIRK: It is all your fault.

SONU: My fault?

MRS. VIRK: If you had spent more time with her, she might have stayed here.

SONU: If you had been more of a mother to her, she might have stayed here.

MRS. VIRK: I am a mother, a good mother. I—

SONU: So you think.

MRS. VIRK (*sniffles*): I wish he was here, to see me suffer like this.

SONU: For once, think about others. For once, did you ask her if she needs anything, for her tuition, her expenses? You have money, don't you, Mother?

MRS. VIRK: Hush, girl, hush!

SONU: You are her mother. You are behaving as if she owes you the world. What have you ever done—

MRS. VIRK (*sniffles*): Not you, too, not you. Do not change on me, Daughter!

SONU: Does it matter to you?

MRS. VIRK (*sniffles*): I am a mother—

SONU: Everything is a show for you, another chance to put on a show, a drama—

MRS. VIRK: Oh, hush, girl.

(*Sonu removes the cushion from underneath Mrs. Virk's foot and hits her ankle with it. Mrs. Virk tries to ward her off with her hand. She grabs the cushion and places it under her foot again.*)

MRS. VIRK (*raising her voice*): Do not change on me! Do not you change on me!

(*Silence.*)

(*Indu brings her suitcases downstairs and rolls them to the side. She returns upstairs.*)

MRS. VIRK (*holding her ankle as if in pain*): Oh.

SONU (*loudly, with exasperation*): Mother, please!

(*Silence.*)

(*Indu returns with her handbag, overcoat, etc., and leaves them at the foot of the stairs. She moves the cushion carefully from under Mrs. Virk's foot. Mrs.*

SCENE NINE

Virk tries to stand up, but sits down as if feeling the pain in her ankle. Indu provides support for her. Sonu nods and walks behind them.

Mrs. Virk folds under Indu's arm support as her foot is entangled under the leg of the coffee table. She screams in pain and sits down on the floor. Sonu shakes her head and sinks into the armchair.)

INDU (*baffled*): Mother! Mother, are you all right? Sonu! Sonu, would you assist me with Mother?

(*Sonu reluctantly gets up to help Indu. Both hold Mrs. Virk by supporting her and assisting her in walking.*

As they are about to leave the stage, Indu returns to pick up her belongings at the foot of the stairs. Sonu and Mrs. Virk are out of sight in the hallway. Indu pauses, looks around, picks up her husband's and father's pictures, and tucks them in her bag. She pauses and looks around once more.)

INDU: At first, I was forced to leave my father's house, and now my husband's...my house, my own house. (*Looking upward*) Oh, you! You have brought nothing but misery to me! (*Pause.*)

SONU (*from backstage, loudly*): Indu, hurry up! I need help with Mother.

(*Indu collects herself and her belongings.*)

INDU (*exasperated*): You owe this fool some luck. And don't you forget that!

(*Indu looks around and takes a deep breath. Sonu enters hurriedly.*)

SONU (*loudly*): Indu, would you bring Mother's jacket. It is in her bedroom. (*She exits.*)

(*Indu is humming a tune. She dashes upstairs to fetch the jacket.*

As she is rushing downstairs, she trips and falls down. She lies motionless at the foot of stairs.

The lights are dimmed and slowly return.

Sonu enters.)

SONU (*mumbling to herself*): At first, you were in a hurry to leave. Now, what is this dilly-dallying? Let us go. (*Looks around and then notices Indu at the foot of stairs. She rushes to her and shakes her.*)

SONU (*frantically*): Indu! Indu! Get up!

(*Mrs. Virk enters. She is limping. When she sees Indu lying on the floor, she walks normally. She looks at Indu and then at Sonu who rushes to the phone.*)

Sonu (*worriedly*): Mother, she is not moving.

(*Sonu is on the phone. She walks away. She is seen but not heard. Mrs. Virk bends over Indu for a moment and watches Sonu who is still on the phone. She picks up her jacket that is entangled under Indu's feet. She shakes it while holding it over Indu to straighten it. Without touching Indu, she walks away and hangs the jacket neatly over the back of the chair. She looks around and sees Indu's belongings. She picks up Indu's bag and goes through it.*)

Mrs. Virk (*to herself*): Look, your father's picture. She is taking your father's picture.

(*Sonu puts the phone down. She begins to speak as she is walking towards Indu.*)

Sonu: I have called the ambulance. (*She is shaking Indu and feels her pulse. Turning towards Mrs. Virk*) Mother, I am afraid.

(*Mrs. Virk continues to go through Indu's bag.*)

Mrs. Virk (*to herself*): She is taking his picture.

(*Sonu walks over to her mother and removes Indu's bag from her lap. She snatches her father's picture from her mother's hands and throws it on the chair.*)

Sonu (*sobbing, angrily*): He is dead! He has been dead for a long time! Look at her. Look at your daughter.

Mrs. Virk: My daughter?

Sonu: Yes. Your daughter, Indu. She is not moving.

(*Mrs. Virk is looking into empty space. An ambulance is heard in the background. Mrs. Virk gets up and picks up Father's picture. Sonu grabs it from her and throws it against the wall. The glass shatters. Voices are heard in the background. Mrs. Virk is picking up the scattered pieces of the picture.*)

Sonu: He is dead. He has been dead for a long time.

VOCABULARY

Kadhi: a dish made out of yogurt and chickpea flour.

Bhua ji: father's sister or father's female cousin.

ABOUT THE AUTHOR

H. K. Jeji is a retired high school librarian and teacher. She enjoys reading, traveling, and spending time with her family and friends. Her published plays, titled *Crossings* and *Warp and Weft of Our Lives*, explore the complex experiences of immigrants adjusting to life in North America.

www.ingramcontent.com/pod-product-compliance
Lightning Source LLC
Chambersburg PA
CBHW022119040426
42450CB00006B/771